Brave
Norman

A True Story

ISBN 0-439-42595-6

Text copyright © 2001 by Andrew Clements. Illustrations copyright © 2001 by Ellen Beier. All rights reserved. Published by Scholastic Inc., 557 Broadway, New York, NY 10012, by arrangement with Simon & Schuster Books for Young Readers, Simon & Schuster Children's Publishing Division. SCHOLASTIC and associated logos are trademarks and/or registered trademarks of Scholastic Inc.

12 11 10 9 8 7 6 5 4 3 2   2 3 4 5 6 7/0

Printed in the U.S.A.   24

First Scholastic printing, November 2002

The text of this book was set in Times New Roman.
The illustrations were rendered in watercolor.

PETS TO THE RESCUE

Brave Norman

A True Story

Written by Andrew Clements
Illustrated by Ellen Beier

SCHOLASTIC INC.
New York Toronto London Auckland Sydney
Mexico City New Delhi Hong Kong Buenos Aires

Steve McDonald wanted
another pet for his family.
He went to an animal shelter.

CATS

PLEASE
Wash hands

Joey

4

He saw many dogs.
He saw many cats.

Then he saw Norman.

Steve said,
"That's the one!"

The shelter people said,
"No one wanted this dog.
We are very happy
you picked him."

So was Norman.

Norman loved his new family.

He loved Steve.
He loved Annette.

He loved little Paul.

And he loved Lucy,
the family's other dog.

Norman followed
Annette and Paul and Lucy
around all day.

He went to the park with them.
And he loved going
to the beach.
But one day Norman
started bumping into things.

The family took him
to the animal doctor.

The doctor said,
"This dog is going blind.
There is nothing we can do."

The family
took Norman home.

Friends said, "Poor dog.
Are you sure you want
to keep him?"

14

Annette said,
"We love Norman.
We will take care of him
no matter what."

It was not always easy
having a blind dog.

He bumped into things.
He was scared of noises.
He barked when people
came near.

Lucy was old and very kind.
She knew Norman
needed help.
Lucy walked close to him.
Then Norman did not
bump things.

Norman still went to the beach.

At the beach,
there were no trees to hit.
There were no cars
to scare him.

Norman ran and ran.

One day Annette and her mom
took little Paul to the beach.
Norman came too.

Suddenly Norman ran off.

He ran into the water
and started swimming.

Then Annette saw something.

A girl was far out in the water.
She was having trouble.
She had called for help.
No one had heard her
except Norman.

The girl kept calling,
and Norman kept swimming.

When Norman got close,
the girl grabbed his tail.

Annette watched Norman.
Norman was helping the girl.
But he was swimming
the wrong way.

24

Annette called, "Norman!
Here boy!"

Norman swam
toward the beach.
He was pulling the girl!

But the girl was very tired.
She let go of Norman's tail.

Norman tried to find the girl.
He swam around and around.

Annette yelled to the girl,
"Call him! His name is
Norman!"

"Norman! Norman!" called
the girl.
Norman came near.
The girl grabbed him again.
This time she did not let go.

Norman pulled the girl
out of the water.
People helped her
onto the beach.

The girl was cold and scared.
But she was safe.

Norman had saved her life.

Norman used to be the dog
that no one wanted.

People used to feel sorry
for Norman
because he was blind.
Now there are books
about him.
He has been on TV.

Being blind did not stop
Norman from being brave.
Being blind did not stop
Norman from helping.

Now Annette is training
Norman to visit hospitals.
Norman can make
children laugh.
Norman can help sick people
feel a little better.

Norman is a true animal hero.